BUILDING A NATION

A NATION UNITED
1780-1850

Written by:
Stuart Kallen

A NATION UNITED

Published by Abdo & Daughters, 6535 Cecilia Circle, Edina, Minnesota 55439

Library bound edition distributed by Rockbottom Books, Pentagon Tower, P.O. Box 36036, Minneapolis, Minnesota 55435

Library of Congress Number: 90-082610   ISBN: 0-939179-89-X

Cover Illustrations by: Marlene Kallen
Inside Photos by: Bettmann Archive

Cover Illustrations by: Marlene Kallen
Edited by: Rosemary Wallner

TABLE OF CONTENTS

CHAPTER 1
A NEW GOVERNMENT

The Three Branches

Even as the first shots of the American Revolution pushed the thirteen colonies into war, Americans began to organize governments. By 1780, all of the colonies had written constitutions. The documents detailed how laws would be made, how taxes would be collected, and how armed forces would be raised. Most of these constitutions divided governments into three parts, or branches. Each branch served a different function.

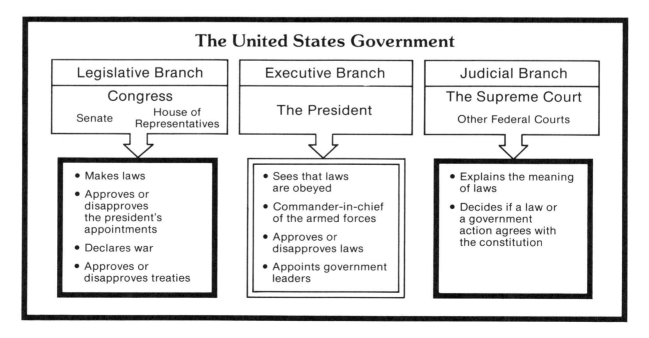

The United States Government

Legislative Branch	Executive Branch	Judicial Branch
Congress Senate House of Representatives	The President	The Supreme Court Other Federal Courts
• Makes laws • Approves or disapproves the president's appointments • Declares war • Approves or disapproves treaties	• Sees that laws are obeyed • Commander-in-chief of the armed forces • Approves or disapproves laws • Appoints government leaders	• Explains the meaning of laws • Decides if a law or a government action agrees with the constitution

The legislative branch made the laws. The representatives in the legislature were elected by the people in their state. To ensure that the lawmakers did not become too powerful, the legislature was divided into two "houses." A bill could only be made into a law if both houses of the legislature agreed to pass it.

The executive branch was headed by the governor. The executive branch made sure that the laws passed in the legislature were enforced.

The judicial branch was made up of judges. The judges explained the laws in court. They also made sure that the laws were carried out equally and fairly.

We, the People of the United States

"We, the people of the United States, in order to form a more perfect Union, establish justice, insure domestic tranquillity, provide for the common defense, promote the general welfare, and secure the blessings of liberty to ourselves and our posterity, do ordain and establish this Constitution for the United States of America."

So states the preamble to the Constitution. In 1790, the Constitution was approved or ratified by all the colonies in America. After many long years of debate, the thirteen separate states were united into one country, the United States of America.

Many ideas were discussed and many compromises were made during the writing of the Constitution. Some people wanted restrictions on voting rights. Some men wanted to outlaw slavery. Most of the men who wrote the Constitution were wealthy merchants and landowners. These men wanted a strong federal government to protect their business rights. The Constitution stated in detail how the government would be run.

The Constitution of the United States was set up like many state constitutions. The executive branch was headed by a president and a vice president. The judicial branch was headed by nine judges who made up the Supreme Court. The legislative branch was Congress. Congress was divided into two branches: the House of Representatives and the Senate.

Each state had two senators in the Senate, no matter how large or small the state. In the House, the number of representatives each state had would be based on the number of people living in the state. People from larger states had more votes in the House than people from smaller states. Each state had equal representation in the Senate.

The Constitution could be changed or amended by two-thirds of the states agreeing to change it. (The Constitution has been amended only twenty-six times since it was written.)

The Bill of Rights

The Constitution could not be approved until all thirteen states agreed to ratify it. Many states did not want to give a federal government power over their rights. For three years, bitter debate raged in Rhode Island as every other state ratified the Constitution. When the writers of the Constitution agreed to add the Bill of Rights to the document, Rhode Island ratified the Constitution in 1790.

In 1791, ten amendments were added to the Constitution. The amendments were known as the Bill of Rights. They guaranteed Americans the right to free speech, freedom of religion, and freedom of the press.

Who Votes?

After the Constitution was signed, Americans had more say in their government than most other countries. But many people in America were not allowed to take part in their government. Only white men who owned property were allowed to vote. This meant that women, blacks, Native Americans, and poor people had no right to vote or serve in the government.

In the late 1700's, women were not allowed to own property. When a woman married, all of her property became her husband's property. But women worked hard to build America. Besides the work of bearing children, women were farmers, innkeepers, brewers, tanners, ropemakers, printers, tinworkers, lumberjacks, woodworkers, bankers, and more.

Abigail Adams tried to gain more rights for women. Abigail Adams was married to John Adams, one of the men who wrote the Declaration of Independence and the Constitution. Although Abigail Adams tried to get her husband to insure women's rights in the Constitution, women did not have the right to own property for another one hundred years.

Women did not have the right to vote for another one-hundred-and-fifty years. Since almost 50 percent of the American population was women, the Constitution ignored one-half of all the people living in the United States.

Blacks were not allowed to vote, even if they owned property. Many states did outlaw slavery. Vermont, Pennsylvania, New York, New Jersey, Connecticut, and Rhode Island outlawed slavery after the Revolution. Even though slavery was against the law in these states, blacks were still denied equal rights and basic freedoms. In states where slavery was legal, blacks had no rights at all.

Native Americans were continually pushed off their land and killed. The Consititution did not apply to them either.

The First President
Now that the United States had formed a new country, it had to prove itself to its citizens and the world. Could such a large country made up of so many different people succeed?

Washington takes the oath of office for the presidency.

On April 30, 1789, in New York City, George Washington was sworn in as the first president of the United States. Washington had been a hero of the Revolutionary War. He had been a guiding force during the writing of the Constitution. But Washington was tired of life in public service and wanted to retire. When his country called, however, Washington took the tough job. While waiting to leave for his inauguration, Washington wrote to a friend that he felt like a "culprit who is going to the place of his execution."

The Constitution allows the president to choose a group of men to help him run the government. These men make up what's known as the Cabinet. Washington chose Thomas Jefferson, Henry Knox, Edmund Randolph, and Alexander Hamilton as his Cabinet when he set up the nation's first presidency.

The Nation's Capital

In 1790, Maryland and Virginia donated sixty-nine square miles of land to the federal government. There, on the swampy banks of the Potomac River, work was started on a city that would be the capital of the new nation.

CHAPTER 2
YEARS OF GROWTH

World Trade

America had run up huge bills paying for the Revolutionary War. When Washington became president, America was 50 million dollars in debt. American money was barely worth the paper it was printed on. Before the war, America could only trade with England. Now that America had won its independence, trade with any country in the world was possible.

In 1790, it was not unusual for a ship to be leaving Boston Harbor bound for China. The ship's cargo might have included New England butter, Philadelphia beer, Rhode Island candles and Appalachian herbs. The ships would return to America with foreign money to help build the nation.

The Cotton Gin

Before the war, England bought all of the rice, indigo, and tobacco that was grown in the South. During the fighting, England found other places to buy those goods. When peace returned, American planters in the South needed a new cash crop.

Inventors in England had introduced machinery that would spin cotton into cloth at a very rapid rate. England's cotton mills were booming because of the new machines. But few Southerners planted cotton. The kind of cotton that grew well in the South had hundreds of sticky seeds in it. Separating the seeds was hard, slow work.

Eli Whitney's Milling Machine.

In the spring of 1793, Eli Whitney, a college student from Massachusetts, demonstrated his new invention. It was called the cotton gin. The cotton gin quickly separated the seeds from the cotton. It could clean 1,000 pounds of cotton a day. Soon plantations all over the South were blooming with white cotton.

Southern cotton production jumped from 190,000 pounds in 1791 to 41 *million* pounds by 1800. With the demand for cotton came the demand for more slaves. Slavery had declined in the ten years after the Revolution. With the introduction of the cotton gin, human slavery began to grow at an alarming rate.

America's First Industry

Grow cotton in the South. Ship it to England to be turned into cloth. Then ship the cloth back to America to be made into clothing. This roundabout process made no sense but America had no choice. The spinning machines that turned cotton into cloth were an English invention. England jealously guarded the secrets of the complicated spinning machinery. It was against English law to sell the machines or the plans. England was the only country in the world that could manufacture large amounts of cotton cloth. That is, until an English factory worker with a good memory decided to move to America.

In 1789, Samual Slater memorized the plans for the spinning machines where he worked in England. When he came to America, he convinced Moses Brown to start America's first cotton spinning mill in Pawtucket, Rhode Island.

In England, children were used to work in the mills. Slater used the English idea of child labor in America. Because of Slater's memory, America became a leader in the world cotton industry.

CHAPTER 3
MOVING WEST

The New Pioneers
Into the setting sun, Americans pushed ever westward. In the early 1800's, the lands to the west were a place of new challenges for the growing nation. Homesteads were given away free to eager farmers. Pioneers could escape the law and the taxes of the East. In 1790, only 4,300 white settlers lived in the Ohio territories. By 1800 over 45,000 had settled there. By 1800, over 700,000 white settlers lived west of the Appalachian Mountains.

A new breed of Americans was settling the lands between the Mississippi River and the thirteen states of the East. Instead of building neat rows of wooden frame houses, pioneers built log cabins. The cabin walls and chimneys were coated with mud. The floors were rough planks. A sheet of greased paper served as a window. In the East, men wore silk shirts and silver buckles. The pioneers wore deerskin pants and shirts with fringe. Money was rarely used in the West. Payment was made with pork, whiskey, hemp and hides. Many of the pioneers were poor people who were snubbed by Easterners. Many people in the East were not happy to share political power and equality with the pioneers. But share they did.

In 1784, Thomas Jefferson wrote a law called the Northwest Ordinance. The law said that as soon as any part of the West had enough voters, it could become a territory. When the territory had enough voters to write a state constitution, it could apply for statehood. Under the new law, Kentucky became a state in 1792. Tennessee became one in 1796 and Ohio in 1803. In 1800, the Harrison Land Act gave the western settlers title to their lands.

Thomas Jefferson, the 3rd President of the United States.

Little Turtle's War

As the settlers moved west and cut down the forests, the Native Americans watched in horror. The tribes in the area had lived there for thousands of years and depended on the forests for their survival. The western territories had become a melting pot of different Native American tribes. Here, the western tribes such as Kickapoo, Sauk, Miami, and Fox, mingled with the tribes of the Iroquois nation who had been driven off their land by American settlers in the East.

In 1790, President George Washington ordered General Josiah Harmar and 1,500 soldiers into Ohio territories to fight the Native Americans. Harmar's trained men were no match for the tribes led by the brilliant Miami chief, Little Turtle. Little Turtle's warriors shot at their enemy and burned their villages to feign panic. They lured Harmar's men deep into Native American Country. Then in two surprise ambushes, Little Turtle surprised the enemy, killing 183.

After several more defeats by the Native Americans, Washington appointed a new general, "Mad Anthony" Wayne. Wayne led 3,000 soldiers against the northwest Native American tribes. In the summer of 1794, Wayne and his men killed thousands of Native American men, women and children. Then he burned their villages and crops.

On August 3, 1795, over 1,100 Native Americans signed the Treaty of Greenville. This treaty gave all of Ohio and Indiana to the United States. Little Turtle, who had believed that the white men could not be defeated, was one of the signers. The surviving Native Americans were packed up and moved farther west.

CHAPTER 4
THE WAR OF 1812

The Louisiana Purchase
In 1801, Thomas Jefferson became the third president of the United States. Two years later, he sent James Monroe to France. Jefferson wanted to buy New Orleans from the French for two million dollars. Monroe returned with a surprise for Jefferson. He had purchased the entire Louisiana Territory for 15 million dollars.

Thomas Jefferson signing the Louisiana Purchase papers.

The Louisiana Territory included all the lands west of the Mississippi River to the Rocky Mountains. The territory stretched from the Gulf of Mexico to Canada. The size of the United States was now doubled.

Renewed Hostilities

At the same time that Jefferson was buying Louisiana, war had broken out in Europe between France and England. Americans had been trading with both countries. The French navy seized any U.S. ships headed for England. The English navy stopped any U.S. ships headed for France. To make matters worse, the English captured U.S. sailors and forced them into the British Navy. Many Americans were outraged.

Jefferson decided to stop all foreign trade in Europe. This lead to great hardships in America. Suddenly, thousands of merchants and farmers had no market for their goods. Before he left office in 1809, Jefferson decided to begin trading again with Britain and France. Once again American ships were seized by the warring nations. This time, the British took more U.S. ships than the French.

To make matters worse, western settlers found out that Native Americans had British guns. Many Americans believed the British were helping the Native Americans fight the U.S. government. On June 18, 1812, James Madison, the fourth president of the United States declared war on England.

James Madison, the 4th President of the United States.

The Western Front

The War of 1812 was fought over a much larger area than the Revolutionary War. The Great Lakes were the sight of many naval battles. In the West, Native American leader Tecumseh urged all tribes to band together to fight the Americans. He had seen his people pushed west and murdered by the thousands. For this reason, Tecumseh sided with the British in the War of 1812. Because of the Native American's help, the British made some great advances. By the end of 1812, the British held the cities of Detroit and Chicago.

War of 1812.

The War in the East

In early 1814, the French surrendered to the British in Europe. Britain was now free to spend all its energy fighting the Americans. In the fall of 1814, the British invaded Washington, D.C. President James Madison, and thousands of other people fled the capital city. The British soldiers marched in unopposed. The British soldiers piled up furniture in the White House and set it on fire. They pulled down the rugs and books in the Capitol Building and set them on fire also. By the end of the day, Washington, D.C., was wrapped in a sheet of flames.

The Star Spangled Banner

On the night of September 13, 1814, near Baltimore, Maryland, the British Navy pounded Fort McHenry with cannonballs. The next morning, the British ships left because they could not get close enough to damage the fort.

Francis Scott Key, an American prisoner of war, was on one of the British warships that night.

After the night of British bombardment, Key saw the United States flag still waving in the dawn's early light. He wrote a poem about the flag waving in the rockets' red glare. Later the poem was turned into the song "The Star Spangled Banner." The song became the national anthem of the United States.

Peace at Last

The war had taken its toll on America. Washington, D.C., had been burned and ransacked. The nation needed 50 million dollars to continue the war, but the government was bankrupt. The British demanded one-half of all American territory as the price for peace.

In October 1814, a full-scale British attack from Canada was repelled on Lake Champlain by thirty-year-old Captain Thomas Macdonough. It was a stunning blow to the British Navy. On Christmas Eve 1814, a peace treaty was signed between America and England. The war had changed nothing, but had cost the United States 127 million dollars and 5,000 lives.

The Battle of New Orleans

News traveled slowly in 1814. While America and England were signing a peace treaty to end the war, Andrew Jackson was getting ready to fight the British in New Orleans. Jackson's army was a ragtag group of soldiers: Tennessee backwoodsmen, Kentucky riflemen, freed slaves, Creoles in colorful uniforms, French soldiers, and even a pirate named Jean Laffite.

Andrew Jackson, leader in the Battle of New Orleans.

On January 8, 1815, the British started the attack. The Americans hid behind rows of logs as thousands of red-coated British soldiers marched towards them. When Jackson yelled "Fire!" row after row of British soldiers fell. Only 21 Americans had been killed. Unknown to Jackson, the war had been over for more than two weeks.

CHAPTER 5
TRAVELING THROUGH THE WEST

Roads Through the Wilderness

After the War of 1812, the western frontier began to grow again. By 1820, one-third of the white people in America lived west of the Appalachian Mountains. The new frontier was booming as thousands of settlers arrived every day. The pioneers came to carve out farms, homes, and cities in the American wilderness.

Transportation was the main problem facing the new settlers. Mail coaches needed roads to get from town to town. Farmers needed roads to move their herds of cattle to the markets in the East. And pioneers who were tired of slogging through the mud on their way west wanted better roads.

In 1811, work was started on a gravel road that would stretch 600 miles through the untamed forests of America. It was called the National Road. The eighty-foot-wide highway ran from the mountains of Cumberland, Maryland, to Columbus, Ohio. By the time it was finished in 1852, the road extended west to Vandalia, Illinois.

Reasons for Moving

The National Road was just one of many roads, or turnpikes, crisscrossing the new frontier. Thousands of people were using them every day. During a six-month period in 1817, over 2,000 covered wagons pushed through Gate No. 2 on the Dauphin Turnpike in Pennsylvania. A family of seven was seen walking from New Jersey to Ohio, pushing their belongings in a wheelbarrow. Old America was breaking up and moving westward in white-topped Conestoga wagons. What had caused this great migration?

Inexpensive land costing only two dollars an acre was reason enough for many families to pack up and move. But there were other reasons. After the War of 1812, America was bankrupt. Paper money was worthless and the British had started to flood the country with cheaply made goods.

This forced hundreds of American businesses to close. Thousands of people were thrown out of work. Many had no choice but to leave their homes and try their luck in the West.

The highway was just the beginning of the journey for many of the travelers. Most of the roads ended at rivers and canals, where many travelers kept pushing westward.

Traveling By Boat

In the early 1800's, transporting goods by wagon was slow and expensive. People needed other methods of transportation to link the East and West. America's greatest natural resources, her lakes and rivers, were there to solve the problem.

In the early 1800's people began to dig canals. At first, these wide shipping channels were just short ditches to guide boats around waterfalls and rapids. Mules, horses, or oxen, on paths next to the canal, pulled the boats through the water.

In 1817, the state of New York started a project that Thomas Jefferson called "madness." The state was going to build a canal. It would be 352 miles long and stretch through the wilderness of New York. The Erie Canal would link the Hudson River with Lake Erie.

The job took seven years, cost seven million dollars, and linked New York City to the grain, lumber, and manufacturing centers of the Great Lakes. For seven years, hundreds of workers using picks and shovels dug a ditch four feet deep and forty feet wide between Albany and Buffalo.

The Erie Canal was an immediate success. By charging a toll to the boats that passed through the locks, the Erie Canal paid for itself in twelve years. The cost of shipping a ton of wheat from Buffalo to New York City dropped from 100 dollars a ton to only 5 dollars. The success of the Erie Canal inspired other states to build canals of their own.

Steam Power

In the early 1800's methods of traveling on water had barely changed since the days of Columbus. For thousands of years, the only way to travel on rivers was downstream. Boats could only be driven upstream by means of sails and towlines. Thirty hardworking boatmen needed three months to travel 1,000 miles upstream between New Orleans and Illinois. The flatboats that were used to transport grain could not be driven upsteam. Once they reached New Orleans, they were taken apart and sold for lumber. Then, the crewmen on the boat had to walk home — one thousand miles!

All that changed in 1807. That was the year Robert Fulton invented the steamboat. On August 16, Fulton's boat, the *Clermont*, made its first run on the Hudson River from New York City to Albany. Hundreds of people gathered to watch. Many folks did not believe that such an invention would work. They called the steamboat "Fulton's Folly." As the *Clermont* chugged down the river with its huge, rumbling paddle wheels spraying water into the air, people fled in terror. The smokestack on the boat belched black clouds and fiery sparks.

The *Clermont* was a success. The 150-mile journey was made in only 32 hours. Soon steamboats, with their rough-and-tumble crew, were a regular sight on the rivers of America. By 1817, a steamboat could sail upstream from New Orleans to Illinois in only 25 days.

Railroads

By the time the Erie Canal opened in 1825, a machine was being tested in England that would someday make canals useless. The machine was a steam locomotive that pulled a line of railroad cars.

In 1827, a group of businessmen decided to build a railroad to link Baltimore, Maryland, with the Ohio River. At first, the Baltimore and Ohio Railroad used horses to pull the railroad cars over tracks. Then in 1830, Peter Cooper, a young inventor, convinced the owners of the railroad to use his steam locomotive to pull the cars. The engine was called a Tom Thumb because of its small size.

On August 25, 1830, Cooper's locomotive was raced against a horse to see which one could pull rail cars faster. The locomotive sped along at 18 miles per hour but broke down. The horse pulled ahead and won the race. Everyone laughed at Cooper's machine. But by 1840, over 3,000 miles of railroad track connected the major cities from New England to Georgia. The era of the "iron horse" was changing the face of America.

CHAPTER 6
EXPLORING THE CONTINENT

Lewis and Clark

In 1804, white people had lived in North America for almost 200 years. But very few of them knew what lay beyond the Mississippi River.

President Thomas Jefferson had heard wild tales from fur trappers. But Jefferson wanted hard facts about the vast unexplored territories of the west. Jefferson chose his secretary, Meriwether Lewis, to lead an expedition into the unknown territory.

Jefferson gave his orders to Lewis: find the source of the Missouri River, cross the mountains, and reach the Pacific Ocean. Islands and rapids were to be located. Weather, animal life, minerals, and furs were to be identified.

Lewis chose William Clark as his partner. On May 14, 1804, Lewis, Clark, and twenty-three men left St. Louis, Missouri. They took mirrors and knives to trade with the Native Americans. The expedition was a struggle from the start. The Missouri River rushed past their boats as the men struggled to push upstream. Rain fell continually. High winds tossed their boats like toys.

The group pushed north and west up the center of the continent. The dense forests and high cliffs gave way to an unending sea of grass. In some places the grass was over six feet high.

Sacajawea guides Lewis and Clark through the Rocky Mountains.

After five months and 1,000 miles, the group settled in for the winter near what is now Bismark, North Dakota. The men stayed with the Mandan Native American tribe. There they met Sacajawea, a Shoshoni woman. Sacajawea had been kidnapped by the Mandan tribe and had lived with them for four years. Her people lived in the territory that Lewis and Clark were about to explore. The explorers asked Sacajawea to join their expedition.

In the spring of 1805, Lewis and Clark started their long journey west. Sacajawea was now their guide. They crossed great prairies and long hills. Along the way they met Sacajawea's tribe. The Native Americans gave Lewis and Clark horses and fresh supplies. Sacajawea led the men through mountain passes and unspoiled forests. They crossed the Snake and Salmon rivers. They built canoes to carry them down the Columbia River. Finally, on November 15, 1805, the Lewis and Clark expedition paddled their canoes into the Pacific Ocean in present-day Oregon.

After spending a hard, hungry winter on the coast, the expedition headed home. On September 23, 1806, the men cheered when they saw the stars and stripes flying over a fort near St. Louis. They had been gone twenty-eight months.

Many people thought they had died. But they all returned safely, bringing with them valuable information about the land, people, and animals of the American northwest.

America became fascinated with the West after reading about the Lewis and Clark expedition. In 1806, Zebulon Pike explored Colorado where he saw the famous mountain that bears his name, Pikes Peak. Pike also went down to Santa Fe, in Spanish territory, where he found gold and silver. Slowly, the mysterious new lands of America were opening up to explorers and development.

The Indian Removal Act
In 1825, about 125,000 Native Americans lived east of the Mississippi River. The five main tribes, the Cherokee, Creek, Choctaw, Chickasaw, and Seminole were known as the "civilized tribes." These tribes lived in Georgia, Tennessee, Florida, North Carolina, Alabama, and Mississippi.

The tribes had adopted the customs of the white men. Many had become successful farmers and businessmen. The Cherokee had built roads, churches, and schools. They published their own newspaper. The Chickasaw had developed a new breed of horse. Many Creek and Choctaw had intermarried with the white people. In Florida, the Seminoles were prospering. Many white settlers were jealous of the Native Americans and wanted to take their property.

The Native Americans had treaties with the United States that granted them the land that they lived on "as long as the grass grows and the water runs." But between 1814 and 1825, whites took over three-quarters of Alabama and Florida, one-third of Tennessee, and one-fifth of Georgia, Mississippi, and Kentucky.

Andrew Jackson played a key role in conquering the Native Americans. When Jackson was a young man, he commanded soldiers that fought and killed thousands of Native Americans. In the later years of his life, as a writer of important treaties, Jackson took Native American land and gave it to white settlers.

In 1830, Andrew Jackson was the seventh president of the United States. Jackson signed into law the Indian Removal Act. The act stated that all Native Americans east of the Mississippi must move to the dry, barren lands of Oklahoma.

The Indian Removal Act was deemed illegal by the Supreme Court because it violated the treaties the federal government had signed with the

Native Americans. Jackson did not care that the act was illegal. Soon, Native Americans were being rounded up and forcibly removed from their homes by the U.S. Army. The Native Americans were leaving a warm climate, fertile farmlands, and forests where their ancestors had lived for thousands of years. They were being moved to Oklahoma, which was a dry, barren territory. The tribes did not know how to survive in the new territory.

The Trail of Tears

In the bitterly cold winter of 1831, over 13,000 Choctaw Indians were the first to be marched west under the Indian Removal Act. Driving ox wagons or straggling on foot, the Choctaw trekked through one of the coldest winters on record. The removal was supposed to have been overseen by the army. But the army turned its job over to private contractors who charged the government high fees. The contractors gave as little as possible to the Native Americans. Food was scarce. There were few blankets or tents. Disease was everywhere. Overloaded boats that were to ferry the tribes across the Mississippi River sank among the ice floes. By the time the Choctaw reached Oklahoma, thousands had died.

In 1836, the Creeks were forced to marched to Oklahoma. The men who resisted were forced to walk hundreds of miles, chained together at their ankles. More than 3,500 of the 15,000 Creeks died on the march. In 1837, the Chickasaw made the journey with the same results. In 1838, over 17,000 Cherokee started the long migration. Four thousand died along the way. Forever afterward the forced journey was known as "The Trail of Tears."

Most white people considered the Indian Removal Act a huge success. Vast tracks of land were opened to the cotton planting slave owners of the South. In December 1838, Martin Van Buren, the eighth president of the United States, said that the removal had been completed "with the happiest effects."

CHAPTER 7
ON TO THE PACIFIC

Westward Ho!

By 1840, the stage was set for a massive migration to the West. The Great Plains had been explored. The South Pass through the Rocky Mountains was open. Now wagons could cross the hazardous mountain range that divided east from west. Word began to flow to the East about rich

Pioneers moving west.

forests, rivers teeming with fish, and beautiful mountains full of beaver, bear, and elk.

Independence, Missouri, was a frontier town where pioneers gathered every spring to make the long journey west. Since the trip was too dangerous to make alone, people traveled together in wagon trains. The pioneers would usually hire a guide to take them through the safest western routes.

A wagon train's pace was very slow. The journey took at least six months. The pioneers faced broiling sun in summer and unbearable cold in the winter. Often, they ran low on food. Animals died and wagons broke. Hostile Native Americans and disease took their toll on the weary travelers. Many lighthearted travelers who left Independence on a lovely spring day found a final resting place on the frozen bank of a lonely river in the West. A folk saying went, "The cowards never started and the weak died along the way."

The Oregon Trail

Most of the families that made the difficult, dangerous journey west went to Oregon. In 1840, Oregon included all of present-day Oregon, Washington state, Idaho, and parts of Montana.

In 1834, several churches sent missionaries to Oregon to teach Christianity to the Native Americans. The Native Americans did not want to learn Christianity, but the missionaries wrote letters to their friends and relatives urging them to move to Oregon. Newspapers printed the letters and often told exaggerated stories about Oregon. Between 1843 and 1845, over 5,000 Americans caught "Oregon Fever." They sold their homes and farms, bought oxen and a wagon, and moved to Oregon.

California

While thousands of settlers headed to Oregon, reports of an exciting new land drifted east. With mountains and deserts, the ocean, green valleys, and a climate that resembled summer all year long, California sounded like a dream come true.

Mexico had ruled California since its independence from Spain in 1821. But there were no courts, no police, no postal service, and no schools. The capital of Mexico, Mexico City, was far away. Life in California existed in a world of its own.

Spain had claims in California as far back as 1520. Spanish Catholic missionaries built a string of missions across the state. The friars who ran the missions either convinced or forced the Native Americans to live on the mission lands. There, they worked as farmhands or sheepherders. The friars converted them to Christianity. By 1820, one-tenth of California's 300,000 Native Americans lived and worked for the missionaries. When Mexico gained control of California in 1821, the Native Americans were treated like slaves. By 1848, over 60,000 Native Americans had died in California because of harsh treatment by the Mexicans.

Americans started arriving in southern California in 1840. They found a scattered population of wealthy Mexican ranchers or "caballeros." The caballeros controlled huge "ranchos" and lived like kings. Many caballeros wore silk vests, velvet breeches, deerskin boots, embroidered jackets and sombreros weighed down with gold and silver. Their rich land bloomed with orchards and vineyards, olive trees, and flower gardens. Many Americans became rich from buying cattle from the caballeros and shipping the cattle east.

The Gold Rush

On January 24, 1848, John Marshall spotted a shiny stone lying near a sawmill in Sutter's Mill, California. Marshall said to his friends, "Boys, I believe I have found a gold mine." Indeed he had. The mill belonged to John Sutter. Sutter and Marshall tried to keep their discovery a secret. But word got out. Soon gold fever spread across the continent. In 1849, hundreds of thousands of people traveled to California to search for gold. People came from the United States, Europe, Australia, South America, and China.

A group of California gold miners.

The population of San Francisco, California, jumped from 1,000 people to 45,000 in one year. Suddenly, the sleepy little town was ridden with crime and disease. The streets became rivers of mud. The hotels were now dangerous and dirty.

Tents and shanty villages sprung up on the hillsides. Fire swept through the ramshackled huts six times in eighteen months. Over 450 ships were abandoned in the harbor as gold hungry sailors became miners overnight. In 1850, there were 1,000 murders in San Francisco but only one murderer was punished.

The city of Sacramento, near Sutter's Mill, had four houses in it when gold was discovered. A few months later, 10,000 people were living there. Prices were driven up by the huge population increase. 10 dollars for a dozen eggs! 150 dollars for a sheet of paper! 10 dollars for a thumbtack!

The Life of a Miner
The first miners to arrive in California found huge deposits of gold. They found it in places that were easy to mine, such as dry gulches and creek beds. In the early years of the gold rush, some men struck it rich.

Within a year, the easy areas for mining were picked clean. Huge and expensive machinery was now needed to dig for the gold located deep in the ground. A large labor force was needed to sift through the tons of dirt. Most miners ended up working for large companies for long hours and low wages.

Most people coming to California did not know that the gold was hard to find. Towns sprung up overnight as miners poured into northern California. The miners gave their towns names like Wildcat Bar, Skunk Gulch, Git-up-and-Git, and Ground Hog Glory.

In time, thousands of miners gave up their search for easy riches and went home. Many people stayed in California and within the next ten years the population of the state tripled.

Minorities in California

Native Americans in California were peaceful and lived in small groups, often numbering a few dozen people. As far as the miners were concerned, Native Americans were in the way of their gold claims. The miners wanted to remove the Native Americans.

By the 1870's only 17,000 Native Americans were left in California, reduced from the 200,000 that had lived there in 1848.

The Mexicans, whose ancestors had lived in California for centuries, were treated as foreigners. Whenever disputes arose over land ownership or mining claims, the California courts ruled against Mexicans. The new settlers simply took over the land.

People from China flooded into California during the gold rush. Hardworking and honest people, the Chinese helped to build the farms, irrigation canals, and railroads that made California a successful state. By working hard, the Chinese were often able to make money on mining claims after miners had abandoned them.

The Chinese customs were unknown to the English-speaking miners. Their appearance was different. The Chinese soon became targets of mockery and abuse. The Chinese helped each other, and soon, many of them became successful in California.

Many blacks were brought to California as slaves to work in the goldfields for their masters. Some free blacks made fortunes in the goldfields. By 1850, over 1,000 blacks lived in California. They were the wealthiest black community in America. But blacks faced the same discrimination in California as they did in the rest of America.

By the time California became a state in 1850, it had the most racially mixed population of any state. Mexicans, whites, Chinese, Native Americans, and blacks all lived in California.

From Sea to Shining Sea

Between the writing of the Constitution and the California Gold Rush, the United States grew at an incredible speed. In 1790, there were thirteen states in the union. Just sixty years later in 1850, there were twenty-nine. America's lands streched from the Atlantic Ocean to the Pacific Ocean and included great riches and bountiful resources.

As great as America was, trouble was brewing over an old problem — slavery. The next twenty years would put the country to an incredible test to change the face of America forever.

INDEX

DATE DUE
